7 Steps To Becoming A Ebay Power Seller
Written by: Demarious Bowens

Printed in the United States of America

First Printing, 2016

Content Unlimited

4801 Cobble Creek Cir

Winston Salem NC 27105

www.365moneyonline.com

The Introduction To Ebay

Ebay is overwhelmingly the most familiar and successful online auction marketplace. This is due to the vision of a San Diego, Ca., resident, Pierre Omidyar, who started the company in the living room of his home in 1995 with the help of Jeff Skoll.

Initially, the two men dealt only in collectible items but felt there was a vast untapped market that they could reach. In 1998, Omidyar and Skoll brought Meg Whitman into the fold. The rest of the story is an example of unimaginable success.

Whitman, who had studied at Harvard Business School and was well-versed in branding at companies such as Hasbro, recruited a marketing staff that had an average 20 years' experience per person.

Their collective vision and passion have paid off wildly. According to the 2014 Forbes 2000 list, eBay is worth $71.01 billion.

Brand recognition is one of the reasons eBay is an excellent venue source for people who want to make money online. Its sheer magnitude of its brand almost ensures that potential customers will visit the eBay website before going elsewhere.

Getting started on eBay is a very easy process. Setting a page up is very nearly intuitive, and easy-to-understand tutorials and detailed instructions abound.

Of course, eBay obviously makes a tidy profit. It is a corporation in the business of making money. Fortunately for its online clients, the company asks very modest fees from the people who use its services.

eBay makes money because its sellers make money. That is what makes it a great online marketplace.

Step #1

Finding Your Niche On Ebay

A niche is important no matter what industry you may be in. Gone are the days when 'jacks of all trades' flourished and thrived; today, consumers are more interested than ever in finding someone who is an expert in their field and can provide the sort of dedicated, laser-focused expertise they're looking for. No one wants to take marketing advice from an accountant, no matter how related the fields might be. The same holds true for eBay.

Finding a Niche: Why it Matters

What is the first difference you notice between successful eBay mega sellers and those who only sell a few items each month? If you pay close attention, it's obvious: the mega sellers specialize in one type of product or market. This isn't an accident.

By finding their niche, the mega sellers set themselves up to become experts in that one particular field. They're able to watch the market and analyze seasonal trends. The mega sellers do not have to worry about wrangling half dozen different suppliers onto one schedule because they only offer one item.

Niches are present even in big business. For example, Nike has the market on shoes. They appeal to a specific group: young, athletic types who want only the highest performance wear. Dawn does the same thing on dish soap. While there are others in their niche, they are the most well-known. Aside from effective marketing and branding campaigns, this is a result of focusing on a niche market.

An example of what not to do is the company Mad Katz. You may know them as a third-party supplier of video game accessories; while they are moderately successful, they offer products for all consoles. In recent years, they have been known for the subpar quality of those products. Had they chosen to focus on one specific console and up their quality, they would see more success than they currently do.

Zeroing in on a niche also makes the marketing easier; instead of trying to appeal to every Dick and Jane out there, you can target your marketing efforts towards the group most likely to purchase your products.

Master the Market

Finding a niche has an additional benefit: it allows you to become master of the market. Instead of trying to figure out sales trends for a wide variety of products, you only have to worry about your specific offerings. If you sale necklaces for teen girls, for instance, you can ignore the sales data for bracelets, necklaces for men, and necklaces for older women. It allows you to have a much narrower area of focus. This not only reduces stress, but increases your efficiency.

Professional Appearance

When you focus on only one target market, you become an expert in it. Expert doesn't mean knowing everything there is to know about the market; it simply means knowing more than your competition, or more than those who are shopping for it. If you can establish yourself as an expert, people will come to you for advice – and subsequently purchase your products. The perception of being an expert is more important than the reality of it; so long as you know enough to provide consistent, quality advice to your customers, then you're over halfway there.

Better Inventory Control

Just like a niche allows you to focus on a specific area rather than a wide range of products, it also lets you focus on controlling your inventory more efficiently. The mega sellers on eBay work with suppliers. Most of the sellers have it set up so the products ship directly from the supplier to the customer when an order is placed. While this process is efficient, it does involve a lot of paperwork and set up. Now imagine doing that for a dozen or more products, each in a vastly different area of industry. It would be an absolute nightmare. By finding a niche, you worry only about one area, and you can keep better track of your sales and inventory, as well as knowing when you should order more based on predictions of future sales. If you run out of stock, it can be a major blow to your profits.

How to Find and Research a Niche

Now comes the fun part: finding the niche. There are a few ways to approach it, but the easiest way is to ask yourself a series of questions:

1. What do I enjoy?

If you focus on a niche you enjoy (for example, selling retro video games) then it will hardly seem like work to get everything set up and running. However, if you focus on something you hate, then every day will be a chore.

1. What do I not want to do?

Everyone has a few things they absolutely despise doing. Even if you could earn money from it, would it be worth it? List the things you cannot stand doing and avoid them whenever possible.

1. What do I have the most experience in?

Leveraging your previous experience can be a great way of finding a niche. What jobs have you worked before? What hobbies do you have? What kind of education? Any area where you might have more experience than the average person is a viable option. If you know a lot about Adwords campaigns, why not write an eBook and market that towards small business owners?

1. What is my target market?

Sometimes you may know the market better than you know an industry. For example, if you're recently out of college, then you understand what college students need and want better than most. From that point, you can work backwards to create something that will appeal to that group.

1. Who could use my services?

Similar to knowing your target market, figure out who could take advantage of what you have to offer. For example, if you have low-cost copywriting services, you could appeal to small business owners and local churches with limited budgets.

Researching the Niche through Terapeak

When it comes down to doing the nitty-gritty research on your niche, you have to look at numbers. Terapeak is a program that lets you gather and collect data on your target market to give you an idea of the profitability of a market. Terapeak allows you to analyze eBay price trends, analytics, seller tools, and listing optimization, all from the comfort of your computer.

It's important to do this research before you fully commit yourself to a niche. While some niches are insanely profitable, others are not. If the audience for a specific niche is not prone to purchasing, or is too small, then your ability to make a profit will be greatly diminished.

Conclusion

There's nothing stopping you from becoming a mega seller on eBay. The process the most successful people have used is completely repeatable; you can mimic every step and see the same success. The key lies in doing the research beforehand and making smart decisions concerning your niche in order to maximize your profitability. Remember, without a niche, success is nearly impossible – but with one, your success stops where your imagination does. Once you get used to the idea of specializing rather than trying to reach all markets, you'll understand why so many choose that path, and then you'll reap the same rewards.

Step #2

Finding Products to Sell on eBay

Now that you have identified a niche that needs filling, you are going to need merchandise to meet your customers' needs. If you have sold most of your household furniture on eBay and are now sitting on the floor, it might be time to consider some other sources for merchandise.

Handcrafted items

If you already have a craft as a hobby, why not make it pay for itself? Handmade soaps are good sellers because they make unique giftable items. In this same vein, you might think about offering baskets full of homemade soaps and handcrafted crocheted or knitted wash cloths. Many parents are turning from using plastic pants for covering diapers to employing old-fashioned knitted woolen soakers, shaped pant-like garments that are made from a renewable resource and that last a long time. Free patterns for these and other articles abound on the Internet. The key to success with handcrafted items is quality workmanship. "Handmade" does not have to scream "homemade."

Distributors

Without an advanced technical degree and a large manufacturing facility, you can still sell the computers and related hardware that other people make. One example is D&H Distributing, headquartered in

Harrisburg, Pa. Companies such as this may have a few major distribution centers scattered across the country and rely on small- and medium-size businesses to make the final delivery of storage and networking solutions, servers and electronic devices. By establishing a relationship with this kind of company, you become a valued reseller. Some may even offer lines of credit for businesses needing capital for expansion. Mobile ordering apps for iPods and iPhones are making this market segment very attractive for small home-based businesses such as eBay sellers.

Drop shipments

Before you have horrified visions of 18-wheelers delivering mountains of cardboard cartons to your house, drop shipments really do not work that way. Instead, you handle the daily details of setting up and maintaining a company's eBay presence, advertising its products, taking orders, collecting payments and forwarding orders to the company headquarters.

The company then sends out its products to the customers. You do not have to invest in any inventory or shipping materials. While you can buy lists of these companies, you can find hundreds of them yourself by conducting your own Intenet search.

Once you have set up a relationship with a company, it is easy to use eBay's built-in shopping cart. Make the payment process easy for your customers by setting up your business to accept credit cards and PayPal.

Liquidation sites and stores

Liquidators, both online and brick-and-mortar stores, are gold mines for the bargain-savvy shopper. You have probably shopped in or have seen stores such as TJ Maxx, Home Goods, Big Lots and Ollie's. Cruise the aisles and look for low prices on quality merchandise in good condition.

Take them home, mark up the price just enough to make a tidy profit and cover your eBay fees. Advertise them separately or in lots at prices that people are willing to pay. Small home décor items, gourmet foods and treats, home textiles, gardening items and tools are only a few categories to consider.

Other online auction sites

This is so easy, it almost feels like cheating.Check out auctions sites other than eBay, grab some great deals and then resell the merchandise.

AuctionOnline.com, Ubid.com, eBid.com and Listia.com are only a small sample of the online auction sites out there. However, these are some of the best. You will need to do some research first.

Visit several sites, watch similar items on eBay and focus on selling items that move quickly. In the business world, the speed at which you move what you are selling is called "inventory turnover."

If your merchandise is not selling, you are not making money. It makes sense to concentrate on items that people want, mark up the prices to reap a nice profit for yourself and cover your ebay fees and then sell them as quickly as possible.

Flea markets and estate sales

You can reap substantial rewards by shopping carefully at these places. Do not be tempted to buy junk at a flea market just because it bears a low price tag.

A dinged-up and rusty item is junk to the person selling it to you, it will be junk to you and it will be junk to the people you are trying to resell it to. On the other hand, there are sometimes real treasures among the trash, so it pays to become very knowledgeable about your specific niche. Estate sales can yield treasures as well, but avoid getting caught up in frenzied bidding and paying too much for something.

You have seen this happen on eBay, and it happens in the brick-and-mortar world as well. Bidding on boxed lots of old items is often a good tactic, because really good things may be hidden beneath the tattered and tarnished items on top. Arrive at the sale early, examine the merchandise carefully and bid wisely.

Garage and yard sales

Items offered for sale at these events often bear price tags that are one-tenth their original purchase prices. Before you are overcome by yard-sale madness, examine the sale items carefully.

Missing parts and pieces are maddening little details that will frustrate your eBay customers if you do not alert them first. Avoid trouble and lost sales. Buy garage and yard sales items that have all their necessary components.

Arrive early for the best selection of merchandise. Arrive late in the day for the best prices. People are often only too glad to rid themselves of unsold items. Even that sad-sack olive-green toaster from the '70s will find a new home if it is in good condition and works when plugged in.

Thrift stores

Thrift stores such as Goodwill and the Salvation Army can sometimes be good sources for potential eBay merchandise. However, they have probably already marked up the price on the merchandise.

You will mark it up a bit more for your own purposes, making its eventual selling price less attractive. Better deals can often be found in community thrift shops operated by charitable organizations.

Household items, particularly vintage textiles and dishes, are often available for a song. Take the articles home, spruce them up a little, put them up for sale on eBay and make a better profit.

Attic, basement and garage cleaning

This is a lucrative way to not only acquire eBay merchandise but also earn extra cash while performing an unwelcome task for someone who cannot bear to get rid of things. Some of these items will most certainly qualify as trash, but you can find treasure if you know what to look for.

Old electrical items such as radios can be taken home, disassembled and the parts sold separately. Auto parts may or not be as profitable.

Boxes of vintage yarn, knitting needles and crochet hooks can be sold in lots or separately. Vintage tablecloths, napkins, sheet, pillowcases and quilts also represent a lucrative category, especially if you market them to people interested in home decorating.

Library and used-book sales

Libraries periodically cull books that have not been circulating well for some time. These are often offered for a song during their annual or semi-annual book sales.

Hardbacks are more profitable for you, the reseller, but do not pass up a unique or much-sought-after paperback, especially if the price tag is 50 cents or less. If you live in or near a college or university town, the American Association of University

Women chapter in the area may hold an annual used-book sale. As with yard sales, arrive early for the best selection or hold out for the final day for the best prices, often a dollar per bag.

You may find other desirable items such as maps and sheet music that collectors will pay top dollar for in some cases.

Dumpster diving

If your town allows it, cruise the streets early on trash pick-up day. Household and automotive items may be setting on the curb, waiting for the trash man to take them away. You will often find gently used items that look almost new.

Other items may require a little elbow grease, but once they have been cleaned up, they will bring surprisingly good prices. Take your truck instead of your SUV, or borrow a friend's, in case you find something large that looks too good to pass up.

In the case of small homemade items and thrift store finds, storage will not be much of a problem. If you have settled on rescuing and reselling furniture and car parts, dedicate one side of your garage or a dry corner of your basement to use as a mini warehouse.

Alternatively, offer to rent space from a friend or family member who has room to spare. In any event, avoid dealing with wholesalers operating from China, such as dhgate.com.

You will have problems, received bad reviews from customers and may eventually have your eBay account shut down. Your ultimate goal is making money on eBay. Avoid a few pitfalls and pratfalls while you are accumulating your inventory.

Step #3

Building a Great eBay Store

Whether you use eBay as a way to make some extra cash, as a hobby, or as a full-time job, there's no denying that eBay stores are the way to go.

While starting an eBay store is not the work of an instant, eBay has made the process as simple as possible for those who want to take the leap. In this chapter, we will discuss some of the most important things to consider when you create your store.

Choosing the Right Name

Picking a name for your eBay store is often trickier than it might seem. You need a catchy title that also contains relevant keywords that will bring your store name to the forefront of any search. Buyers want to be able to find the items they need quickly. Before you begin contemplating names, you will first want to identify your target audience. Who are you trying to sell your products to? As with any other business, the goal is conversion. You want more people to view your store and you want a large percentage of those individuals to actually make a purchase.

The following are some tips to keep in mind that will help you to both increase your eBay store traffic as well as conversion rate:

- Use keywords that are pertinent to your products

- Choose a name that has an available domain name (we'll discuss this more later)
- Pick an interesting title that is easy to remember

Registering a Domain Name

Once you have determined what you want to name your store, you will want to make sure that your title has an available domain name. You can look this up easily using sites such as GoDaddy.com. Reasonably priced, these websites allow you to check the availability of your domain name as well as register your domain. This will allow you to appear more professional and established to your clientele and will also improve your online visibility. Additionally, you can use it as a part of your marketing by attaching it to all of your flyers, online ads, newsletters, and emails.

Importance of Creating an Affiliate Website

One of the biggest mistakes made by eBay store owners is not creating an affiliate website on which to sell their products. Chances are, more than one visitor will be interested in buying each of your products. However, once that item is gone, it's gone. What happens to the rest of your visitors who wanted to purchase the item? If they can't find it with you, they'll look for it somewhere else. To prevent the loss of a potential customer, create a website!

Since you already have a registered domain name,

creating a website could not be easier. All you need is a reliable hosting option and you are up and running! Not only are websites easy to make, they can also do wonders for your conversion rate and your overall profits and success.

While eBay does not permit users to directly link to their site on their Sales Page, the company has no problem with you providing such a link on your About Me Page. All you have to do is mention on your Sales Page that more information about your products can be found on your About Me Page. Simple as that. Now your customers can further explore your store and you won't miss out on any sales.

Designing Your Logo

Customizing your eBay store is both crucial as well as a lot of fun! When it comes to designing your store's logo, the most important thing to keep in mind is to make it as attractive and unique as possible. While you can spend a significant amount of time and money creating a design, there is a easier way to go about it.

eBay provides you with four basic templates that you can use. While the options are certainly limited, this can be a great choice for store owners who are not experienced in creating custom online storefronts.

To create a simple, effective logo, combine a catchy title with a graphic that directly relates to the items that you will be selling. With your logo, you want to make your store's purpose clear to visitors before they even enter the store itself.

To create an image, you can utilize one of the many easy-to-use programs out there, such as Adobe Illustrator or Photoshop. There are also sites that you can use online that allow you to create quick logos without much hassle.

When choosing the appropriate text, the most important thing is to make sure that your title will be legible. Do not choose a fancy font that will be difficult to read. Far too many first time eBay store owners make the mistake of creating a fancy logo that might look impressive but is far too difficult to read in thumbnail form.

Selecting a Theme

Once you have created a logo, you will need to further customize your store by choosing a unique theme, or aesthetic, for your page. Your theme will typically consist of your store header and footer, your navigation bar located on the left of your page, and your store page navigation.

With eBay, you can choose between predesigned themes that are simple to implement, and customizable themes that will take some more time, but will create a more unique look for your store.

Experiment and have fun with this. If you are new to themes, consider beginning with a predesigned theme. Once you become more familiar with your store and with your clientele, you can further customize your theme at a later time.

Properly Using Keywords and Meta Tags for Search Engine Optimization (SEO)

Search engine optimization is crucial to the success of any store, and your eBay store is no exception. Two critical aspects of SEO are keywords and meta tags.

We touched on keywords before. You want to pick keywords that users are likely to search. Make the most of this. Do a little research before selecting your keywords. See what keywords are commonly used and integrate them into your page. This will greatly increase your odds of increasing traffic to your site.

Meta tags are another useful tool that you can utilize to further optimize your site. Essentially, meta data serves as a summary of the data that is present on your page. It is specifically designed to attract search engine spiders.

While meta tags are not displayed as a part of your page's image, they act as a way to reinforce your keywords and attract search engine queries.

Opt-In Newsletters

Keeping potential and current customers informed about your store is a crucial part of marketing. Opt-in newsletters are a great way to achieve this. The difference between opt-in newsletters and other emails is that the customer chooses to receive them.

They can unsubscribe at any time, making your customers feel in control of what they do and do not receive. Without being unnecessarily annoying, these newsletters allow you to provide your customers with interesting information and encourage them to make repeated purchases at your store.

Make sure that you only provide information of interest. Don't just repeat news, since this is a good way to get blocked. Include things like sales, new product information, and the like. Sending out these newsletters is incredibly easy with eBay's email marketing system. This tool is offered as a part of your store ownership.

In addition to electronically sending out your newsletters, send a print-out with each purchase you mail out. Doing so will increase your credibility and make your customers feel as if they are getting something for free. Who doesn't love that?

Keeping Yourself and Your Buyers Informed with RSS Feed

Really Simple Syndication, or RSS, is a programming format that allows you to refresh your content without having to take the time to make manual updates.

Many RSS Readers are free to use and can be easily downloaded. Once you have a RSS Reader, all you need to do is copy your feed address into the Reader you downloaded and that's it. The Reader will notify you whenever your URL is updated.

Your eBay store can benefit greatly from this handy tool. Using RSS feed, you can easily inform buyers about any updates to your products and inventory as well as keep yourself up-to-date on the status of your auctions. RSS can be easily enabled under your Store Marketing tab.

Use Cross-Promotions to Your Advantage

A great way to further hone your eBay store is to take advantage of cross-promotions. Essentially, cross-promotions allow your buyers to see other items that they might be interested in when they look at and/or purchase your products.

EBay allows you to set up relationships between your items by entering certain keywords. This will determine what your buyer sees, and can increase your sales and traffic dramatically.

In Conclusion

Along with being able to take advantage of increased free listings and customizable options, eBay store owners can also enjoy increased web traffic and business success at a reasonable price. Not only this, but eBay stores are far more likely to attract visitors and retain the long-time loyalty of buyers.

Step #4

Secrets to Selling Like Mad On Ebay

As the top site for amateur and a professional auction on the Internet, eBay has attracted a great deal of attention for its ability to help people sell, sell, sell. There are, however, so many people who are attempting to do the same things at once that it can be difficult for an individual to find a way to get the job done.

eBay can be quite frustrating without the right strategy. Here are the tips that you need in order to sell like mad on eBay.

First, you must label your product correctly using a long tail title.

Nothing is moving on eBay without the proper listing from the very beginning, so make sure that you pay special attention to this tip.

What exactly is a long tail title?

A long tail title is a title that is full of special, localized and precise keywords that will attract a specific type of person to your listing. In order to sell the most products on eBay, you must make your product the most visible.

In order to be the most visible, you must be seen in the major search engines as well as within the internal eBay search engines as high on the list as possible. The long tail keyword is essential to this strategy.

The difference between a long tail keyword and a regular keyword is what?

For instance, if you are selling a towel on eBay, you do not want to title your listing "towel." You will be relegated to the back pages of the search engines, your product listing will not get very many views and you will not be able to attract a higher price for your wares.

However, if you listed your towel according to its defining characteristics, you will stand out from the crowd. The people who see your listing will know exactly what they are seeing.

Any person who clicks through will likely be highly interested in what you have to offer because they would not have clicked at all otherwise! The search engines will also be much more likely to list your product in a high space according to the keywords that you have chosen.

Instead of listing your towel as "towel," you could try "White Marriott Towel Signed by Jack Nicholson." This is a long tail keyword.

This listing defines your towel as unique, setting it apart from all of the other towels that are being sold on eBay.

Of course, you should only list your towel this way if it has actually been signed by Jack Nicholson! The purpose of this example was to ensure that you find the defining characteristics of your merchandise and list it as your keyword.

Second, make sure that you have more than one high quality picture of your merchandise.

This is an especially important tip if you are a new seller on eBay; however, it is also important even for established sellers. It is very easy and cheap to get a high quality picture of your product, so just take the time to do it.

If you do not have a camera or a smartphone that takes HD pics, invest in one. You will be able to use it for the remainder of your time on eBay. The additional offers that you will attract will pay for the investment within your first few sales.

Every seller on eBay has also been a consumer at one point or another, so it should be easy to sympathize. Remember the thoughts that you had when confronted with a poorly presented product.

You did not even want to try it out - you were too taken aback that the seller did not even have enough confidence or wherewithal to give the product a proper presentation before expecting you to buy it.

If you have a less than perfect picture, your potential buyers are looking at you the same way! Remember that no one really knows how well your product works except you; you cannot expect people to read your mind. Present your product with HD pictures so that others can see what you see.

Third, create a great description and use terms

from the site of the manufacturer.

Taking the time to create a great description is the same concept as taking the time to make sure that your pictures look right on the site. If you do not do this, then the potential buyer will be immediately put off by the lack of professionalism. Additionally, a great description allows the buyer to recognize what he or she will be getting. Make it shine!

Using descriptions from the manufacturer's website is also a great idea. It creates brand continuity that helps a potential buyer to feel comfortable when making a purchase.

Second, they have already done the market research that details the phrases that work best with customers. Why would you not take advantage of the millions of dollars that have already been put into consumer research?

Fourth, price your wares competitively.

Price research is essential to making a great impression on eBay. If you price your products too high, of course you know what will happen: The potential customer that might have made a purchase from you will instantaneously move to another seller.

Lower prices are easy to find both on and off eBay: There are functions in the search engine that give the customer the ability to search for low prices directly. Do your research to make sure that you are competitive.

However, if you set your price too low, you may actually get less sales, especially if you are selling a product that people associate with luxury or performance. A price that is too low will set off suspicions of an incomplete or broken product. The customer will not ask you these things: He or she will simply move on to a price that is more trustworthy. Do not be the lowest price in the book unless you can justify it in the description.

Consider the shipping fee when you price your item. Compare your prices to prices on eBay and factor in any Paypal fees that are associated with the purchase as well.

Fifth, ship globally if you can.

A wider distribution means more potential customers. This is fairly self explanatory.

Sixth, make sure that you list in at least two categories.

Not everyone looks up items the exact same. You need reach for people who may find your item through a secondary keyword. Find related terms to your keywords and put your item in at least two relevant categories.

Seventh, use social media for wider exposure.

The more eyes that you get on your listing, the more potential sales you will be able close. Use your social media links to get these eyes on your product. Popularity never hurt a seller.

Eighth, close out your professional performance by sending the buyer an invoice immediately and thanking him or her for the purchase.

If you want your buyers to come back, make sure that you leave them with a good taste in their mouth after they hit the "buy" button. Send them an invoice and let them know how they can get in touch with you if they have a problem with their purchase. This action alone will ensure fewer complaints.

If you follow all of the tips above, you are sure to get more buyers and more return customers on your eBay listings. There are no shortcuts when it comes to keeping a customer happy. Good luck and happy selling!

Step #5

The Proper Steps to Shipping on EBay

Ebay is a forum that allows people to virtually connect with others from around the world. Acting as a seller on eBay requires attention to detail and a thorough understanding of the shipping process.

Failure to adequately ship items could lead to low rankings and, ultimately, closure of the storefront.

Provide Free Shipping or Determine a Price to Charge Costumers

The first step is to determine how you will send your items to customers. You have two choices; you can either choose to ship the items at no cost to the customer, or you can list a shipping fee with the product.

Sellers are responsible for the cost of shipping if the shipping is offered to buyers for free. When you select your shipping service, you will click the "Free Shipping" box.

To calculate the cost of shipping for items, you will enter information such as the dimensions of the package, the size of the package and the type of shipping into the "Calculated: Cost Varies by Buyer" segment.

This feature will also take into account the buyer's zip code, and the program will calculate the shipping for you. Working to reach a price attractive to buyers is of utmost importance.

How to Save on Shipping with eBay and Flat Rate Shipping

Having a true shipping scale at home will ensure that you always enter the proper weight for the items. Minimize the cost to you with the maximum benefits.

While you want to choose the proper packing materials to get the items there in perfect condition, you do not need to spend a lot of money on these items.

If a buyer needs another item because the first one is destroyed, you will spend more in shipping in the long-term. Furthermore, look for the lowest-priced shipping option available.

Choosing a flat race box, for example, as much as you can keeps the cost down for customers. Priority mail generally costs more than a flat rate box; however, you should still compare the costs to know for sure.

Depending upon the other factors in the equation, priority mail might be more suitable. However, you may be surprised at all that flat rate shipping can contain. Flat rate shipping is often suitable for both small and medium items. Consulting with the officials at your local post office is useful at least when you are getting started.

Using eBay Shipping Labels

Ebay works in-conjunction with PayPal to offer you an efficient and easy way to create labels. Some stray away from this idea because they think they need special labels, but with this system, you can simply print them on regular paper and attach them to the boxes.

Other features available when you use eBay to create shipping labels include tracking information, delivery confirmation, signature confirmation, the ability to manage labels and the ability to create multiple labels at the same time.

Through the same service, you can also schedule a drop-off or a pick-up for the packages. You will have to pay for the labels, but purchasing them through this service is less expensive than doing so at the post office.

Additionally, you don't have to drive to the post office and spend time waiting in a line just for labels. You can pay through your PayPal account without even having to sign-in, and they will be delivered right through your printer.

The lower the process costs for you, the better prices you can offer to your customers and the more business you will be able to generate.

Getting Paid Faster When Using a Tracking Number
Once the goods are in the works to being on route to the customer, you want to ensure that you are paid in a timely and efficient manner.

If you offer a tracking number on your goods, then buyers are going to know exactly when their items are going out. They will have more confidence in you as a seller. Offering tracking numbers means that the buyer can see when the package leaves and when it is on the way to them.

Furthermore, they will also know when the package has been delivered. These tracking numbers help to protect both you, the seller, and the buyers by offering up-to-date information on where the goods are.

In order to add tracking numbers, you can go into the "Sold" section of your eBay account.

Once there, you will click on "Add Tracking Number" button, and you will simply type in the tracking number.

You may also be asked to provide the name of the carrier if the system is unable to determine it with the information that you provide. Providing tracker numbers can also help to get you higher reviews and, therefore, more customers.

Shipping Supplies: Scales, Bubble Wrap, Boxes, Etc.

Failure to have an adequate amount of shipping supplies in your home could mean that you are unable to send products in a timely fashion.

This could result in low ratings and fewer sales. Furthermore, you might be rushing out to get supplies at the last minute and spend more than you would need to if you had been prepared. You can order your shipping supplies directly from eBay itself, so all of your transactions occur in one place. A shipping scale can be purchased in an array of places, but be sure it is a reliable model.

Otherwise, you could end up miscalculating the shipping costs to someone's financial detriment on a regular basis. You are also able to order shipping supplies directly from the United States Postal Service or the United Parcel Service's websites.

By going to the Help Center on eBay, you can click a link that says "Order free US Postal Service Priority Mail boxes." Stocking your house with shipping supplies is easy and efficient with this tool.

How Shipping Cost Plays a Part in What Your Item Should Be Selling For

Shipping on eBay is a major part of the process. While displaying attractive photos of the item and constantly checking into your account are necessary parts of the process, shipping is the way that items actually arrive at their destination.

The most important part of shipping is ensuring that it is done accurately, effectively and in a timely fashion. However, you also need to understand how shipping costs play a role in what your item should be selling at.

 For example, if you are offering free shipping, then you likely need to factor the cost of shipping into the price of the item. Otherwise, you are going to lose money on all of your sales.

Still though, you need to consider cost from the buyer's end. Many people are looking to get the most for their money, so if an item has an outrageous shipping cost, then they might not be interested in the product at all.

Consider an item that is selling for $2.00 but has a shipping cost of $5.00. Customers are often unwilling to pay more for shipping than for the item itself because they do not feel it is worth it.

However, they might be fine with paying $5.00 or $6.00 for the item itself with free shipping. Part of accurately pricing items when it comes to shipping involves thinking like a customer.

Learning how to ship properly on eBay is crucial. Once you have mastered the fundamentals, you can get packages to your customers in a short amount of time, and you will be able to really expand your business on this massive online storefront.

Step #6

Customer Satisfaction is Key on Ebay

To truly stand out as an exceptional seller on eBay, auctioneers must showcase a competitive edge by providing impeccable service during each step of every transaction.

The cornerstone of a prosperous store in this online venue revolves around placing a dedicated emphasis on astute customer service. This chapter explores the nuanced duties that advanced sellers can perform to continuously trounce their marketplace rivals.

Happy Customers Equal More Money

Focusing on consumer satisfaction facilitates long-term relationships with repeat buyers. The benefits of happy buyers are innumerable, but the main advantages include droves of positive ratings, repeat purchases and word-of-mouth advertising. A sense of mutual satisfaction will keep an eBay store fluidly expanding and thriving.

Describe Products Truthfully

An accurate overview is essential for trust to be built among a customer base. Never build expectations that cannot be met by excessively hyping the item or exaggerating features. Be as straightforward as possible to confidently rise above the effusive praise that competing sellers use to stuff their listings with vague glorification.

An overabundance of sales jargon will dissuade casual collectors, so attuned sellers decidedly pinpoint the attractive qualities of an item without delving into endless extrapolation. Keep in mind that blanket generalizations open the door for petty customer disputes, so a finite focus on specific details is completely worth the effort in the long run. Being real will save the trouble of having to explain inaccuracies to the seemingly mechanical site administrators.

Be Honest & Sell Quality Products

At the bottom line, pure honesty is always the best policy. Back up all claims with clear item images to prove the veracity of all listings. High definition photos of the items will instill perfect accuracy for every listing.

If a product needs to be tested for functionality before being sold, make sure to conduct the trial in advance of a listing being posted. The offering of broken items should be avoided at all costs, especially in instances of "Buy It Now" sales.

Revoked sales can lead to bad feedback, but it is still better to absorb the dissatisfaction up front. Remember, smart sellers never ship damaged goods knowingly, and they always explicitly mention the exact condition of every object in their store regardless of value.

As a side note, the appearance of too many "Good" and

"Acceptable" items may cause potential buyers to devalue a store's merchandise in its entirety.

Stave off a reputation for poor quality by maintaining a stocked supply of items within the categories of "Very Good," "Like New" and "Brand New."

These three descriptors should typically form the majority of a shop's inventory with few exceptions. The rarity of an item can sometimes offset a lesser condition, so keep this in mind when assessing each offering on its own merit.

Offer Discounts When Possible

Savings dramatically boost the appeal of an eBay store, especially when positively compared to similar offerings. If the current market for a product is down to the wire in terms of competitive pricing, a small percentage discount will instantly make a listing the most affordable one on the site; therefore, even the subtlest difference counts! Take advantage of a dwindling pool with slight slashes.

Another route for wise sellers often centers on incentivized bulk purchases to boost their sales with ease. A standard way to implement this strategy is to include a threshold for purchases that grants a free bonus, rebate or shipping discount.

Everyone is irresistibly compelled by free shipping, and surprise mailing upgrades work wonders. Surprisingly, enhanced shipping services can also be more inexpensive. For example, Parcel Post can be replaced by

First Class Mail for qualifying items to increase speediness and reduce cost.

Promo codes can also cultivate viral marketing with steep cuts for shrewd buyers. Witty text bolsters the widespread impact by delivering substantial savings steeped in humor. This method creates a brilliant avenue for rewarding frequent customers for their extended patronage.

Be Quick Responding to Questions and Inquiries

Promptness demonstrates a high level of care that makes customers feel personally important, which in turn generates an increased likelihood for future purchases. Speedy communication is an excellent venue to rapidly illustrate sincerity and attentiveness, which instantly garners a sense of security among customers.

After receiving an immediate response to an inquiry, buyers will subconsciously imply that their items are beings shipped in the same keenly quick manner. Sometimes, a thorough response can even motivate them to preemptively leave a good review before their item even shows up!

Leave Positive Feedback

Customers will have ample gratitude for sellers that leave good ratings immediately after payment has been tendered. Kind feedback builds a foundation for positive exchanges in the future. With this perspective, it is wise to avoid withholding feedback as collateral; aside from being impolite, this maneuver sends the signal to buyers that something is likely to be wrong with the item. The misconception will be generated well before the item arrives at their location, which means they will have the entire wait to expect a defect.

This misconception can cause them to look for a flaw in a perfectly fine item, so it is best to completely avoid this possibility by leaving stellar scores from the beginning.

Give Free Samples to Repeat Customers

Every purchase reveals a buyer's personal interests, and clever auctioneers can appeal to each consumer's niche proclivities by including additional items of relevance in the package. Make sure that these add-ons are lightweight to avoid incurring unnecessarily massive shipping charges.

These thoughtful inclusions will increase the potential for receiving positive feedback, and they can attract return purchases right away. A free gift may spur desire for similar products, and customers will also be intrigued by the anticipation of little freebies in the future.

As a bonus, this method is useful for clearing smaller items from an inventory to make room for bigger selections. If the bonus materials are already too small to sell on their own, the costs of this technique are completely absorbed from the start as a means of simple liquidation.

Supply Shipment Status

Precise estimates for shipping ranges are known to be universally appreciated by customers eagerly anticipating the date of their purchase's arrival. Tracking numbers graciously provide confirmation of a buyer's parcel, which fosters peace of mind during the transition period of an online transaction.

Provide insurance options to induce further mental ease for clients. Stave off the need for costly replacements by using sturdy packing materials. After quality, fast delivery is the main desire of most purchasers.

In a similar vein, exaggerated estimates should be avoided; instead, extend the shipping windows slightly to make the item look like it showed up early.

Follow Up

Many sellers unfortunately act like the deal is done at the moment they place the box in the mail, but this is simply not the case. Auctioneers that can stand by their products will have no problem confidently reaching out to buyers after they have received their items.

This is the cherry on top of the customer service cake. Contact all clients to make sure the product meets their standards. Go above and beyond by requesting a complete performance review, and implore about any bonus gifts if they were included. Asking what could be improved in the future is a calculated way to respectfully value a customer's choice to conduct business with a certain store. By making every buyer feel important, an eBay seller will ascend the ladder faster than the crowd can conceive.

Chapter Recap

Happiness Becomes Profit:

A thrilled customer will be inclined to return, and they will gladly spread attention to other interested shoppers.

Truthful Overviews Make Happy Buyers:

Being true to life with item descriptions delights customers by providing a viable alternative to in-store observation. If the item does not match, future purchases are out of the question, and it may even be subjected to the site's return policies.

Item Quality is a Foundation of Success:

An observable trend for mostly top-notch products is advised for drumming up serious recognition. Strict assessment standards weed out less profitable merchandise to ensure the company's reputation remains in the realm of premium offerings.

Discounts Drive Sales Up:

The notion of price reductions is guaranteed to attract financially savvy shoppers. There are a variety of ways to introduce discounts, and they can be easily adapted to a wide variety of niche stores. Techniques include free shipping, coupon codes and batch price cuts.

Quick Question Responses Make a Difference:

Fast attention is the most surefire method to show customer's an invested interest. Thoughtful responses to all posed inquiries should be given as soon as humanly possible. This helps maintain their interest while assuring them of pristine service.

The Role of Positive Feedback:

Leaving good feedback right away encourages healthy consumer relations all around, and it nudges buyers to leave similar positive reviews.

The Benefits of Free Samples:

Giving freebies to recurring customers acts as an invitation for future store visits, and it makes them feel intrinsically valued by the seller.

Introduction to Safe Shipping:

Be exact with the shipping window, or leave time to buffer delays. Offer plenty of options for nuanced customer needs.

The Power of the Follow-Up:

Seal the deal with a polite follow-up to spur return visits and fine-tune services.

Step #7

Ebay Bookkeeping and Inventory Control

Whether you are just starting your Ebay business or you are interested in taking it to the next level, you may understanding that tracking your inventory is a critical component for success.

Your inventory is the lifeblood of your business. When you only have a few items in your inventory, it may be easy to remember relevant inventory information such as the sales price you paid and the price the item was sold for through Ebay.

However, in order to be a truly successful Ebay seller, you will need to turn over a considerable amount of inventory for a profit, and it is not possible to remember all the finite details of each product that you buy and sell. There are a few different solutions that you can employ for improved bookkeeping and inventory control.

The Importance of Tracking Your Inventory For Tax Purposes

There are several key reasons why you need to track your inventory as an Ebay seller. Practically, the IRS will require you to submit detailed, accurate information on the value of the inventory you are holding as well as on the acquisition price and sales price of the items that you sold during the tax year.

Tracking this information can be difficult without an effective bookkeeping and inventory control system. Furthermore, you will need to track other business-related expenses, such as office supplies, mileage and home office expenses.

How Tracking Inventory Boosts Profits
While tracking inventory may be required for tax purposes, it also is important for other reasons. Even if you have only sold a few items on Ebay so far, you may have noticed that some items sell more quickly and generate more interest than others.

These hot items are items that you may want to focus on as you expand your business. When you track inventory regularly, you can more accurately determine how well different items sell.

You can also analyze the data for specific information, such as which items sell better seasonally and which items may generate a greater profit.

After all, some items may sell quickly, but the profit margin may be smaller. Other items may take a longer period of time to sell, but you may generate greater profits.

In addition, by tracking this information, you can make better decisions about how much to purchase items for and the starting bid price on Ebay. Altogether, tracking inventory and improving bookkeeping practices can help you to more effectively and successfully run your Ebay business.

Basic Inventory Control and Bookkeeping System

Many Ebay sellers will begin to use an Excel spreadsheet when starting their business.

A spreadsheet is a simple option to consider, and you can create columns that indicate the dates you bought and sold the items, product descriptions, the cost of the items as well as the sales price and the profit.

When you are managing a small selection of items, this is a manageable solution to consider. However, even if you only turn over a few items per week, but the end of the year, your spreadsheet may have several hundred entries or more.

It may be difficult to fully review and analyze the data in a spreadsheet even for smaller Ebay businesses. Likewise, it can be challenging to analyze the spreadsheet when preparing your taxes.

Altogether, an Excel spreadsheet may be functional, but it may not be as effective as other solutions available to you.

More Advanced Solutions

Regardless of the size of your Ebay business, it makes sense to consider utilizing a more advanced inventory control and bookkeeping solution.

There is a cost associated with investing in some inventory control and tracking software programs, but the cost is typically more than recouped rather quickly.

Some of the free online programs may be effective for you, but they may lack functional features that ultimately may benefit you.

There are several popular programs on the market today, and many are online programs. These include EasyAuctionsTracker.com, StitchLabs, McLane Logistics Technology's Inventory Management, Shopseen.com and others.

What to Look For in an Inventory and Bookkeeping Program

All Ebay business owners may benefit from a software program or online solution that has inventory tracking features and basic bookkeeping features like generating profit and loss statements.

Almost all of the programs you will find have these features, including the free programs online. However, some offer additional features that ultimately can enhance your ability to conduct business and manage finances.

For example, some will track all of your expenses, including mileage. This makes it easy prepare your taxes at the end of the year.

Furthermore, some will generate reports for you that help you to determine which inventory has been sitting in your stock for a long period of time, which inventory generated the greatest profit and other details.

As a business owner, it is cost advantageous for you to have access to this information because it enables you to make better decisions. While you can pull this information from an Excel spreadsheet, you may find that it is less time-consuming and more effective to use a software program.

Using Your Inventory Control and Bookkeeping System Most Successfully
It is not enough to simply find a great inventory control and bookkeeping system. In order to maximize the benefits that a fully functional program can provide to you, it needs to be utilized regularly.

Information will need to be inputted into the system regularly and accurately. Furthermore, you will need to use the system to generate reports. In turn, you can consult the reports when making business decisions.

When used most effectively, you may rely on the data from your system to make buying decisions when restocking your inventory as well as when determining a starting bid price for your items.

It can be stressful, confusing and even costly to attempt to run an Ebay business without an effective inventory tracking and bookkeeping system. Because of this, all Ebay business owners should spend time reviewing the options. With several solutions available, the fact is that there is a system that likely can facilitate improved efficiency and profitability in your company.

Chapter Summary

When you run an Ebay business, the key to success and

profitability is directly related to your ability to control your inventory successfully. From understanding which items to stock your inventory with to making sound decisions regarding inventory costs and minimum bids, there are several factors that you will need to track and analyze in order to run your business with success. From basic Excel spreadsheets to free online programs and paid software programs, there are many choices available for inventory tracking and bookkeeping. Ebay business owners should review the features, costs and benefits of each solution in order to find the right option for their use.

www.ingramcontent.com/pod-product-compliance
Lightning Source LLC
Chambersburg PA
CBHW070411190526
45169CB00003B/1208